CONTENTS

WHAT IS A CABLE?

You already know what a cable looks like. A group of stitches that looks like a plain rib suddenly twists and becomes more like a rope. Or, several groups of stitches cross over each other and look woven or even knotted. These are all cables. Many knitters are intimidated by cables but they shouldn't be—cables are easy to knit once you understand the basic technique. Quite simply, a cable is created by knitting groups of stitches out of order.

Imagine you have four stitches on your left needle that you are getting ready to knit. From right to left the stitches are numbered 1 through 4. As you are knitting, you take stitches 1 and 2 off your left needle to wait safely (without dropping!) and place them onto a cable needle. While those stitches are out of the way and on the cable needle, you knit stitches 3 and 4 from the left needle. Next, knit stitches 1 and 2 off the cable needle. What you've done is change the order in which two groups of stitches have been worked—stitches 3 and 4 first, followed by stitches 1 and 2.

Where you keep the stitches waiting on the cable needle determines the direction that the cable crosses. If you keep the cable needle in front of your work while you knit the next (out of order) stitches off the left needle, then the cable will cross in a left direction. Conversely, if you put the cable needle behind your work, then the cable will cross in a right direction.

In addition to the direction that a cable slants, it can vary in other ways.

- The number of stitches in a cable can vary from two to 12 or more. You can put as few as one stitch on the cable needle to as many as six or even eight.

- The number of rows that are worked between the cable crossing can vary. In a simple, classic, interpretation of a basic cable, the stitches and rows are balanced. For instance, a cable of eight stitches will cross every eighth row.

- A cable can go straight up and down on your knitting or it can travel—the entire cable can move—diagonally.

- In addition to trading places, knit stitches and purl stitches can change.

LEFT = FRONT
RIGHT = BACK
Use a trick in order to commit
this rule to memory
(LEFT my car in FRONT...
be RIGHT BACK).

You don't need to be an expert knitter to master cables. To get started, you really only need to know how to knit and purl. It's helpful to understand some basic characteristics of cables.

- Usually, cables are created out of knit stitches with purl stitches on either side. Because the knit stitch is higher than its purled-stitch background, it accentuates the cable.

- Cables draw the knitting together from side to side.

- Cables add density and therefore warmth to your knitting.

- Expect to use more yarn to cover the same area with cables compared to basic stockinette stitch.

TOOLS

Cable needles are available in many shapes, materials, and sizes but they are all pointed on both ends. Some are straight with either a dip or a bump in the middle (even a short double-pointed needle will do). Others have a short handle with a 'U' shape at the end, like a fish hook. Cable needles can be made from metal, plastic, or wood. In addition, cable needles come in several sizes based on the diameter of the needle. The bulkier the yarn, the bigger the cable needle you will need. However, your cable `needle should always be smaller in diameter than your knitting needle, otherwise you might stretch your stitches. The type you use is a personal choice. Try a few different needles; you'll soon decide which type you prefer.

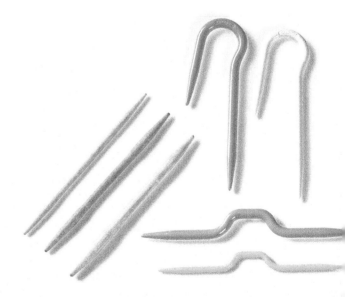

CHARTS

A knitting chart is a graphic format used to visually represent each stitch in a piece of knitting. Each square on the chart represents one stitch and each line of squares represents one row of knitting. Symbols for knitting stitches or directions are placed inside of the squares. Think of the chart as a road map. If you need to know how to drive somewhere you can either look at a map (the chart) or read the written directions for each turn (just like row-by-row knitting directions).

Read the chart from the bottom to the top. The first row of your knitting is represented by the first row of squares on the bottom of the chart. The last row of knitting is represented by the squares on the top of the chart. Odd numbered rows are right side (RS) rows and even numbered rows are wrong side (WS) rows. Each row is read horizontally before progressing up to the next one. So far, pretty easy but now you need to pay attention. Right side rows on the chart are read horizontally from the right to the left. Wrong side rows on the chart are read horizontally from the left to the right. If you are making a piece of knitting comprised of six stitches and eight rows then you would read the chart as follows:

Row 8 (WS)	1 2 3 4 5 6 →	
	6 5 4 3 2 1	Row 7 (RS)
Row 6 (WS)	1 2 3 4 5 6	
	6 5 4 3 2 1	Row 5 (RS)
Row 4 (WS)	1 2 3 4 5 6	
	6 5 4 3 2 1	Row 3 (RS)
Row 2 (WS)	1 2 3 4 5 6	
	6 5 4 3 2 1	← Row 1 (RS)

> CHARTS FOR KNITTING in the round are always read from right to left for every row (that's because you are always working on the right side, the public side, of the knitting).

Starting at the bottom right corner, the numbers in the squares on each row represent the order in which the stitches are to be worked before progressing up to the next row. It helps to understand the exact meaning of right side and wrong side. The right side is the public side, what is seen on the outside of a garment. The wrong side is the private side, the side that is worn next to your body and not seen. Knitting charts depict the work from the right side, the outside of your work. The projects in this book are knit back and forth.

SYMBOLS

Symbols are placed into the squares on a chart to indicate how a stitch or group of stitches should be worked. As you know already, the majority of knitting is created by using either the knit stitch or the purl stitch. The gold standard of knitting patterns is the stockinette stitch, which is knit on the right side (RS) and purl on the wrong side (WS). The 'symbol' to represent a knit stitch on the right side is actually a blank box that looks like this: ☐ Remember that each square of a chart represents a single stitch. The blank box means to knit that particular stitch on the right side and purl it on the wrong side.

A chart to represent Stockinette Stitch looks like this:

A chart to represent Stockinette Stitch looks like this:

The directions for the chart read as follows:

Row 1: Knit.

Row 2: Purl.

Rows 3 – 8: Repeat rows 1 – 2 (3 times more).

Row 8 (WS)
Row 7 (RS)
Row 6 (WS)
Row 5 (RS)
Row 4 (WS)
Row 3 (RS)
Row 2 (WS)
Row 1 (RS)

The symbol to represent a purl stitch is a horizontal line and it means purl on RS, knit on WS.

Combining the two symbols to make a rib results in this chart:

Directions

Row 1: K2, p2, k2, p2.

Row 2: K2, p2, k2, p2.

Rows 3 – 8: Repeat rows 1 – 2 (3 times more).

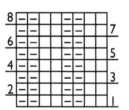

Some helpful information about using charts:

• Read all the directions and look at the entire chart before you start a project. The charts and directions are helpful companions. If you don't understand a step in the directions or an area on the chart, you can often figure it out by using the companion.

• Photocopy the chart and enlarge it.

• The cable symbols in this book are a different color but you might find it helpful to develop some other color keys to keep track of your knitting. For instance, highlight the wrong side rows, or the background stitches.

• Develop a system to keep track of the row you are working in the chart. Use removable highlighting tape, put tick marks next to the row in the chart, or move a ruler up the page. A row counter can also be helpful.

• Charts actually look very much like your knitting. The plain boxes mimic the flat aspect of a knit stitch while the horizontal line symbol for a purl looks very much like the horizontal bumps of an actual purl stitch. Likewise, you can easily detect the shape and size of a cable in the chart. Use this as another tool.

• Charts and knitting directions are not always perfect. Learn to think for yourself and notify the publisher if you find a mistake.

The stitch legend on page 5 explains in detail what each symbol means.
Mark this page in your book because you will refer to it often.
Or make a photocopy of the page for easy reference.

STITCH LEGEND

☐ Knit on RS, purl on WS

⊟ Purl on RS, knit on WS

⬤ Make Bobble (MB) - (page 17)

◪ K2tog in knit stitches;
P2tog in purl stitches

◪ SSK

◎ Yarn Over (yo)

3-St RKC Slip next stitch to cable needle and hold at back of work, knit next 2 stitches from left needle, knit stitch from cable needle

3-St RPC Slip next stitch to cable needle and hold at back of work, knit next 2 stitches from left needle, purl stitch from cable needle

3-St LKC Slip next 2 stitches to cable needle and hold at front of work, knit next stitch from left needle, knit 2 stitches from cable needle

3-St LPC Slip next 2 stitches to cable needle and hold at front of work, purl next stitch from left needle, knit 2 stitches from cable needle

4-St RKC Slip next 2 stitches to cable needle and hold at back of work, knit next 2 stitches from left needle, knit 2 stitches from cable needle

4-St RPC Slip next 2 stitches to cable needle and hold at back of work, knit next 2 stitches from left needle, purl 2 stitches from cable needle

4-St LKC Slip next 2 stitches to cable needle and hold at front of work, knit next 2 stitches from left needle, knit 2 stitches from cable needle

4-St LPC Slip next 2 stitches to cable needle and hold at front of work, purl next 2 stitches from left needle, knit 2 stitches from cable needle

5-St RC Slip next 3 stitches to cable needle and hold at back of work, knit next 2 stitches from left needle, slip next stitch from cable needle back to left needle and purl it, knit remaining 2 stitches from cable needle

5-St RPC Slip next 2 stitches to cable needle and hold at of back of work, knit next 3 stitches from left needle, purl 2 stitches from cable needle

5-St LPC Slip next 3 stitches to cable needle and hold at front of work, purl next 2 stitches from left needle, knit 3 stitches from cable needle

6-St RKC Slip next 3 stitches to cable needle and hold at back of work, knit next 3 stitches from left needle, knit 3 stitches from cable needle

6-St LKC Slip next 3 stitches to cable needle and hold at front of work, knit next 3 stitches from left needle, knit 3 stitches from cable needle

6-St RC Slip next 4 stitches to cable needle and hold at front of work, knit next 2 stitches from left needle, slip next 2 stitches from cable needle back to left needle, pass cable needle with remaining 2 sts to back of work, purl 2 sts from left needle, knit next 2 sts from cable needle

7-St LKC Slip next 4 stitches to cable needle and hold at front of work, knit next 3 stitches from left needle, knit 4 stitches from cable needle

8-St RKC Slip next 4 stitches to cable needle and hold at back of work, knit next 4 stitches from left needle, knit 4 stitches from cable needle

8-St LKC Slip next 4 stitches to cable needle and hold at front of work, knit next 4 stitches from left needle, knit 4 stitches from cable needle

8-St RIB RC Slip next 4 stitches to cable needle and hold at back of work, (k1, p1) twice from left needle, (k1, p1) twice from cable needle

8-St RPC Slip next 4 stitches to cable needle and hold at back of work, purl next 4 stitches from left needle, knit 4 stitches from cable needle.

8-St LPC Slip next 4 stitches to cable needle and hold at front of work, knit next 4 stitches from left needle, purl 4 stitches from cable needle.

9-St RKC Slip next 4 stitches to cable needle and hold at back of work, knit next 5 stitches from left needle, knit 4 stitches from cable needle

16-St RC Slip next 6 stitches to cable needle and hold at back of work, slip next stitches to second cable needle and hold at front of work, knit next 6 stitches from left needle, purl next 4 stitches from front cable needle knit next 6 sts from back cable needle

KNITTING CABLES

The variables in a cable are: the direction of the cross, the number of stitches involved, and whether the stitches are knit or a combination of knit and purl. The charts and directions below and on the next few pages explain all of these variables, from the easiest to more complex. The directions and photographs walk you through and show you how it's done. Grab some needles and medium-weight yarn, and practice these cable techniques.

FOUR-STITCH LEFT KNIT CROSS
4-ST LKC

These simple cables are made exclusively from knit stitches and they travel straight up and down to form a twisted column or rope. One of the easiest cables to learn is a four-stitch cable that crosses every fourth row. The symbol looks like this and the abbreviation is 4-St LKC. There's a lot of information contained in the box with the blue symbol. The box is four squares wide (this is easy to tell when used in a grid) so you know the cable involves four stitches. The blue symbol inside the box makes an X. The heavier, unbroken line in front points to the upper left, which tells you that the cable will cross to the left. To make that happen, you will need to put the cable needle with the out of order stitches in the front of the knitting. The directions will say, "hold at front of work."

When working cables, there are usually several set-up rows before the cable begins. Work rows I and 2 of the pattern and repeat them a couple times. Then begin following the chart, beginning with row I.

Cast on 12 stitches.

When working cables, there are usually several set-up rows before the cable begins. Work rows I and 2 of the pattern and repeat them a couple times. Then begin following the chart, beginning with row I.

Row I: P4, k4, p4.
Row 2: K4, p4, k4.
In a standard pattern, this is how the directions for Row 3 would appear:
Row 3: P4, 4-St LKC, p4.

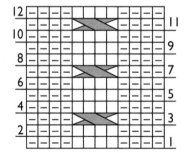

Here's what the directions mean:

1 Purl four stitches then move the working yarn to the back of your knitting as if you were getting ready to knit. Transfer the right needle to your left hand and hold it lightly behind the left needle so that you have easy access to the stitches on the left needle. With the cable needle in your right hand insert the left point of the cable needle into the front of the next two stitches on the left needle as if you were getting ready to purl them.

2 Slide these stitches off the left needle and onto the cable needle. You now have two stitches that should be resting in the middle section on the cable needle.

3 Drop the cable needle and just let it hang loosely, holding two stitches in the front of your knitting.

4 Put the right needle back into your right hand. Working behind the cable needle, knit the next two stitches on the left needle.

5 Tuck the left needle between your fingers so that you can hold the left needle and the cable needle at the same time.

6 Slide the two stitches that are waiting to the right side of the cable needle. Use the right needle to knit these two stitches off of the cable needle.

IT IS PERFECTLY normal, even expected, that your first attempts at creating cables will feel awkward and slow. You will wonder how you could possibly make an entire garment with cables if your first cable took five minutes. I promise that this will get easier. Besides, that's what the swatches in the book are for—practice!

7 Complete the row by purling the last four stitches.

Row 4: K4, p4, k4.
Row 4 is identical to Row 2. Even though the middle stitches have a cable crossing, they are still knit stitches on the right side and purl stitches on the wrong side. They will feel tight and crowded but this is normal; purl the middle stitches just like you did on Row 2.

Row 5: P4, k4, p4.
Row 6: K4, p4, k4.
You have now added 3 rows of knitting after the first cable crossing. Since the cable is crossed every fourth row it's time to cross again. This is how the directions will appear in a standard pattern:

Row 7: P4, 4-St LKC, p4.
Row 8: K4, p4, k4.
Rows 9 – 12: Repeat rows 1 – 4.

You have just created a cable by knitting two groups of stitches out of order. You put two stitches on a cable needle to wait out of the way while you knit the next two stitches from the left needle. Then you pulled the two stitches that were waiting across the front by knitting them from the cable needle.

FOUR-STITCH RIGHT KNIT CROSS
4-ST RKC

This cable is just like the first one except for the direction it crosses. The heavy, unbroken line of the X points to the right, so you put the cable needle with the held stitches behind the knitting, and the cable will cross to the right instead of the left.

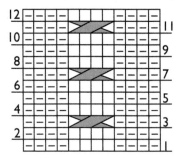

Cast on 12 stitches. Using the chart above, knit the first two rows as follows:

Row 1: P4, k4, p4.

Row 2: K4, p4, k4.

In a standard pattern, this is how the directions for Row 3 would appear:

Row 3: P4, 4-St RKC, p4.

Here's what the directions mean:

1. Purl the first four stitches. Leave the working yarn in front. Transfer the right needle to your left hand and hold the needles so that you have easy access to the stitches on the left needle. With the cable needle in your right hand, reach in from behind the knitting to transfer two stitches from the left needle to the cable needle. Make sure to insert the cable needle into the stitches as if you are getting ready to purl.

2. Drop the cable needle and allow it to hold the stitches behind your knitting. Now, move the working yarn behind the left needle to get ready to knit, but keep the yarn in front of the cable needle. With the right needle back in your right hand, knit the next two stitches from the left needle.

3. Holding the left needle and cable needle together in your left hand slide the two held stitches to the right point of the cable needle. Use the right needle to knit these two stitches from the cable needle (you'll need to scoot the working yarn behind the cable needle).

4. Complete the row by purling the last four stitches.

Now complete the chart.

Row 4: K4, p4, k4.

Row 5: P4, k4, p4.

Row 6: K4, p4, k4.

Row 7: P4, 4-St RKC, p4.

Row 8: K4, p4, k4.

Rows 9 – 12: Repeat rows 1 – 4.

EIGHT-STITCH LEFT KNIT CROSS
8-ST LKC

If the directions call for an 8-St LKC, you knit it just like a 4-St LKC except you cross four stitches in front instead of two stitches. Also, for a balanced cable, you will knit seven rows between cable crossings instead of three rows.

When you reach the cable row:
1. Knit to the location of the cable crossing and slip four stitches to the cable needle, inserting the cable needle into the stitches as if to purl. Hold the needle at front of work.

2. Knit four stitches from the left needle. Knit the held stitches from the cable needle. As you can see, this cable is exactly like the four-stitch version only it's wider.

THREE-STITCH LEFT KNIT CROSS
3-ST LKC

The numbers of stitches crossing do not need to be equal. For instance, you can make a three-stitch cable.

When you reach the cable row:
1. Slip next two stitches to the cable needle and hold at front of work.

2. Knit next stitch from left needle (just one stitch!).

3. Knit two stitches from cable needle.

THREE-STITCH RIGHT KNIT CROSS
3-ST RKC

When you reach the cable row:
1. Slip next stitch to cable needle (just one stitch) and hold at back of work.

2. Knit next two stitches from left needle.

3. Knit stitch from cable needle.

FOUR-STITCH LEFT PURL CROSS
4-ST LPC

You can also make cables that move diagonally across your knitting. For example, in the Dancing Circles on page 25, a four-stitch cable splits into two smaller bands that move diagonally and then join new cables. Remember that most cables are composed of knit stitches surrounded by a purl-stitch background. This type of cable is accomplished when the knit stitches and purl stitches trade places. These cables are called either a Left Purl Cross or a Right Purl Cross.

Just like Knit Crosses, Purl Crosses can be composed of an even or odd number of stitches. The specific directions in the Symbol Legend (page 5) will specify how many stitches to put on the cable needle and which order to knit and purl.

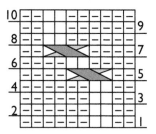

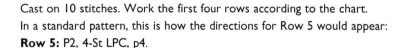

Notice that the symbol is different: the wide band in front, indicating the direction of the cable, is still blue but the two arms in back are grey. **When you see a bi-color cable symbol like this it means that purl stitches are involved.**

A sample chart for this type of diagonal cable looks a little different. In this case, a rib is going to move over four stitches to the left; the knit stitches are going to trade places with the purl stitches.

Cast on 10 stitches. Work the first four rows according to the chart. In a standard pattern, this is how the directions for Row 5 would appear:
Row 5: P2, 4-St LPC, p4.

Here's what the directions mean:

1. Purl the first two stitches then slip the next two stitches to a cable needle and hold in front of your work. Here's where it gets tricky: purl the next two stitches from the left needle.

2. Knit the two stitches from the cable needle.

3. Purl the remaining four stitches in the row. The knit stitches have shifted two stitches to the left.

Row 6: K4, p2, k4. Be a little careful since the position of the knits and purls has changed.
Row 7: P4, 4-St LPC, p2. Work the cable just like row 5.

Work the last three rows according to the chart.

FOUR-STITCH LEFT PURL CROSS AND FOUR-STITCH RIGHT PURL CROSS

4-ST LPC AND 4-ST RPC

Cables that travel diagonally can be combined to form honeycombs, diamonds, even X's and O's. Experiment by working this little chart.

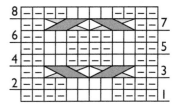

Cast on 12 stitches.
Row 1: P4, k4, p4.
Row 2: K4, p4, k4.
Row 3: P2, 4-St RPC, 4-St LPC, p2.

Here's what the directions mean:

1. Purl two stitches. Slip the next two purl stitches to cable needle and hold in back of work.

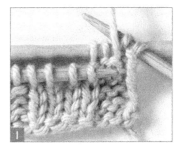

2. Knit two stitches from left needle, then purl two stitches from cable needle to complete the 4-St RPC.

3. Slip the next two knit stitches to cable needle and hold in front. Purl the next two stitches from the left needle then knit the two stitches from the cable needle. You've shifted four purl stitches to the center of the cable.

For the next three rows, work the stitches in the new pattern that's been established.

Row 4: K2, p2, k4, p2, k2.
Row 5: P2, k2, p4, k2, p2.
Row 6: K2, p2, k4, p2, k2.
Row 7: P2, 4-St LPC, 4-St RPC, p2. This is the mirror image of row 4.

You will shift the purl stitches back to the outside of the cable—all the stitches are now in their original places.

Row 8: K4, p4, k4.

EIGHT-STITCH RIB RIGHT CROSS
8-ST RIB RC

Sometimes, all the stitches in a cable are worked in rib stitch. This produces a reversible cable. To work this cable:

1. Slip 4 stitches on the cable needle and hold in back, just like a standard eight-stitch right cross. Work the next four stitches on the left needle in rib stitch: K1, p1, k1, p1.

2. Work the stitches from the cable needle in rib stitch: K1, p1, k1, p1.

3. Continue working both the wrong side and the right side of the cable stitches in rib stitch.

FIVE-STITCH RIGHT CROSS
5-ST RC

Think of this cable as a four-stitch right knit cross with an extra purl stitch in the middle.

1. Slip three stitches to the cable needle and hold at the back of the work. Knit two stitches from the left needle (so far this is just like a 4-St RKC).

2. Move yarn between needles to the front. Slip one stitch from the left side of the cable needle back onto the left needle.

3. Still keeping the cable needle behind your knitting, use the right needle to purl the stitch that you just placed on the left needle.

4. Move yarn between the needles to the back. Knit the two stitches from the cable needle.

KNOTTED CABLES

There are two knotted cables used in this book. In both cases, purl stitches move straight up the work with knit stitches crossed behind. The purl stitches look like the knot that holds a bow together. Although the concept is the same for both cables they are accomplished differently.

SIX-STITCH RIGHT CROSS

6-ST RC

▮1▮ Slip four stitches to the cable needle and hold them in front—this breaks the rule because the cable is a right cross. You will move the cable needle behind after you use it to help make a knot. Knit two stitches from the left needle.

▮2▮ Slip two stitches from the left side of the cable needle back onto the left needle.

▮3▮ Pass the cable needle with the remaining two stitches between the needles to the back of your work.

▮4▮ Move the yarn between the needles to the front. Purl the next two stitches from the left needle.

▮5▮ Move the yarn between the needles to the back. Knit two stitches from the cable needle.

16-STITCH RIGHT CROSS
16-ST RC

To make this cable you will need two cable needles.

1 Slip six stitches to the first cable needle and hold the stitches at the back of your work. Slip four stitches onto a second cable needle and hold in front of your work—these are the stitches that will form the purl knot in front of the knit cross.

2 Knit six stitches from the left needle. This step will feel awkward because you are working between the two cable needles.

3 Purl four stitches from the front cable needle. You'll have to give these stitches quite a tug and also move them to the right side of the cable needle. Also, since you are purling, be sure to move the working yarn in front of the cable needle.

4 Knit the six stitches from the back cable needle. The knitting will feel very tight and crowded but the stitches will loosen up on the next few rows. The stitches on the left needle could accidentally slip off at this point. To avoid that, push the stitches that are on the left needle well away from the tip.

5 When you work the first wrong side row after the cable crossing it's difficult to distinguish the center stitches, which are to be knit (after being purled on the front side). Pay careful attention to the directions and chart for the wrong side rows, and don't forget to count!

ADDITIONAL TECHNIQUES

To make the projects in this book you need to know a few techniques in addition to knit and purl.

INCREASE ONE STITCH
INC 1 ST

1. If increasing into a knit stitch, first knit in the usual way but don't take the new stitch off the needle. Pivot the right needle to the back of the left needle and insert it knitwise (from front to back) into the back loop of the same stitch you just worked. Make another knit stitch in the back loop.

   Slip the old stitch off the left needle. Now you have two stitches in place of one.

2. If increasing into a purl stitch, first purl in the usual way but don't take the new stitch off the needle. Keeping the working yarn in front, pivot the right needle to the back of the left needle and insert it purlwise (from the back to the front) into the back loop of the same stitch you just worked.
   Make another purl stitch in the back loop.

   Slip the old stitch off the left needle. Now you have two stitches in place of one.

MAKE ONE INCREASE
M1

1. If you pull your knitting from side to side you'll notice that a little ladder is formed between the stitches. Insert your left needle from front to back under this ladder.

2. You now have a new loop on the left needle. To give this new stitch an extra twist, knit into the back loop (the loop furthest away from you).

KNIT TWO TOGETHER DECREASE ⊠
OR PURL TWO TOGETHER DECREASE
K2TOG OR P2TOG

The symbol for this decrease is the same regardless of whether it is being worked into knit stitches or purl stitches. In either case you work two stitches at the same time.

K2tog: Insert the right needle knitwise (from front to back) into the next two stitches on the left needle. Knit these two stitches at the same time as if they were one stitch. You have just decreased by one stitch.

P2tog: Insert the right needle purlwise (from back to front) into the next two stitches on the left needle. Purl theses two stitches at the same time as if they were one stitch. You have just decreased by one stitch.

YARN OVER ▢
YO

Wrap the yarn over the needle creating a loop that will be worked as a new stitch on the next row. The yarn over leaves a distinctive hole in your knitting and is often used decoratively. Yarn overs are worked differently depending on whether you are knitting or purling.

Knit: Bring the yarn forward and lay it over the right needle in a counterclockwise direction ending behind the two needles. Knit the next stitch. Notice that the yarn has made an extra loop on the needle.

Purl: Keeping the yarn in front, wrap it counter-clockwise around the right needle. Purl the next stitch. Notice that the yarn has make an extra loop on the needle.

SLIP, SLIP, KNIT ⊠
SSK

This decrease is very similar to a K2tog except that the decrease is knit through the back loops of two stitches at the same time. Working one at a time, slip two stitches to the right needle as if you were going to knit them (knitwise). Insert the tip of the left needle into the front loops of these two stitches.

Now your right needle is in the back loops of the two stitches that are being decreased. Knit these two stitches at the same time through the back loops as if they were one stitch. You have just decreased by one stitch.

MAKE BOBBLE ◉
MB

(K1, yo, k1, yo, k1) all into the next st, turn, purl 5, turn, knit 5, turn, p2tog, p1, p2tog, turn, slip 1, k2tog, pass slip st over.

Bobbles are created by 'stalling' on the stitch where you want the bobble to be. You increase many times into that single stitch and then knit back and forth on the newly created stitches. Finally, the bunch of stitches is decreased back to one stitch. Here's how:

1. Work up to the stitch where you want to place the bobble. Knit the stitch and draw the yarn through to the front but don't remove the stitch from the left needle.

2. Yarn over by moving the yarn forward between the two needles and then lay it over the right needle in a counterclockwise direction.

3. Knit into the same left stitch again but still don't remove the stitch from the needle.

4. Work another yarn over. The last step is to knit one more time into the left stitch but this time remove the old stitch from the left needle. Notice that you have five new stitches coming out of the single stitch that you just took off the left needle.

5. Turn the knitting so that you are looking at the wrong side. Purl just the five new stitches.

   Turn the knitting again so you are looking at the right side. Knit the five loops.

6. Turn the knitting again and work some decreases as follows: purl 2 stitches together, purl 1 stitch, purl 2 stitches together.

7. Turn the knitting back to right side and work the last set of decreases as follows: slip 1 stitch to the right needle as if you were going to knit it, knit the next two stitches together, then pass the slipped stitch over the knit stitch and off the end of the right needle (just like binding the stitch off).

8. Continue across the row as directed in the pattern. When you reach the bobble stitch on the wrong side, work it as the single stitch shown in the chart but make it a very tight stitch.

BASIC CABLE

The basic cable is a building block for more complex cables. The number of stitches in a basic cable can vary from two to 12 or more. In addition, the number or rows that are worked in between the cable crossing can vary. In the most simple, yet classic, interpretation of a basic cable the stitches and rows are balanced. For instance, this cable is eight stitches wide and it is repeated every eight rows.

BASIC PATTERN
Multiple of 8 stitches with 4 edge stitches *(optional)*

RIGHT SLANTING CABLE
(8-ST RKC)
As shown on left side of swatch
Row 1 (RS): P2, k8, p2.
Row 2: K2, p8, k2.
Row 3: P2, 8-St RKC, p2.
Row 4: K2, p8, k2.
Row 5: P2, k8, p2.
Row 6: K2, p8, k2.
Row 7: P2, k8, p2.
Row 8: K2, p8, k2.
Repeat rows 1 – 8.

☐ Knit on RS, purl on WS
⊟ Purl on RS, knit on WS
▨ 8-St RKC

8-St Repeat

LEFT SLANTING CABLE
(8-ST LKC)
As shown on right side of swatch
Row 1 (RS): P2, k8, p2.
Row 2: K2, p8, k2.
Row 3: P2, 8-St LKC, p2.
Row 4: K2, p8, k2.
Row 5: P2, k8, p2.
Row 6: K2, p8, k2.
Row 7: P2, k8, p2.
Row 8: K2, p8, k2.
Repeat rows 1 – 8.

☐ Knit on RS, purl on WS
⊟ Purl on RS, knit on WS
▨ 8-St LKC

8-St Repeat

BAMBOO CABLE

If you want to add some interest to a basic cable, vary the number of rows between the cable crossings. The result looks like bamboo.

BASIC PATTERN
Multiple of 4 stitches with 4 edge stitches *(optional)*

☐ Knit on RS, purl on WS
⊟ Purl on RS, knit on WS
▨ 4-St RKC

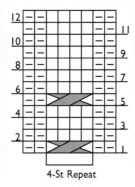

4-St Repeat

Row 1 (RS): P2, 4-St RKC, p2.
Row 2: K2, p4, k2.
Row 3: P2, k4, p2.
Row 4: K2, p4, k2.
Row 5: P2, 4-St RKC, p2.
Row 6: K2, p4, k2.
Row 7: P2, k4, p2.
Row 8: K2, p4, k2.
Row 9: P2, k4, p2.
Row 10: K2, p4, k2.
Row 11: P2, k4, p2.
Row 12: K2, p4, k2.
Repeat rows 1 – 12.

SIMPLE SERPENTINE CABLE

By pairing right and left crosses above each other in a column, you create a serpentine cable. This is a fun and lively cable that is easy to knit.

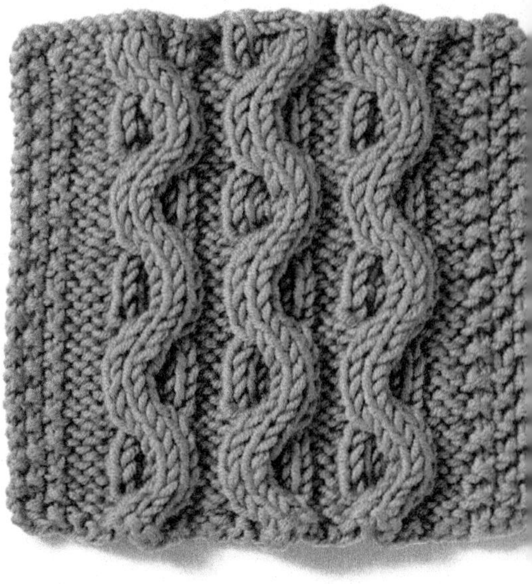

BASIC PATTERN

Multiple of 6 stitches with 4 edge stitches *(optional)*

Knit on RS, purl on WS
Purl on RS, knit on WS
6-St RKC
6-St LKC

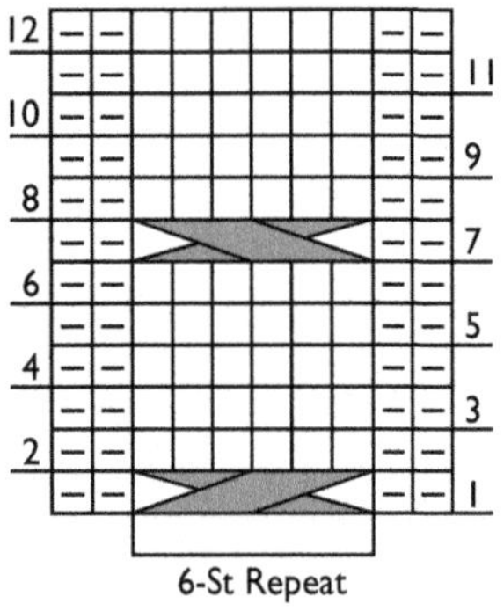

Row 1 (RS): P2, 6-St RKC, p2.
Row 2: K2, p6, k2.
Row 3: P2, k6, p2.
Row 4: K2, p6, k2.
Row 5: P2, k6, p2.
Row 6: K2, p6, k2.
Row 7: P2, 6-St LKC, p2.
Row 8: K2, p6, k2.
Row 9: P2, k6, p2.
Row 10: K2, p6, k2.
Row 11: P2, k6, p2.
Row 12: K2, p6, k2.
Repeat rows 1 – 12.

SQUIGGLES AND BUMPS CABLE

This fun cable introduces two new techniques: Bobbles and purl cross cables. Bobbles (page 17) are raised balls of stiches, created by increasing several times in a single stitch and then knitting back and forth on the newly created stitches. Purl cross cables (pages 10 and 11) use knit and purl stitches together and are very effective in creating diagonal lines.

BASIC PATTERN
Multiple of 6 stitches with four edge stitches *(optional)*

☐ Knit on RS, purl on WS
⊟ Purl on RS, knit on WS
⊡ MB
▨ 3-St RPC
▨ 3-St LPC

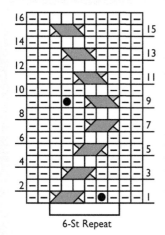

6-St Repeat

Row 1 (RS): P3, MB, p1, 3-St RPC, p2.
Row 2: K3, p2, k5.
Row 3: P4, 3-St RPC, p3.
Row 4: K4, p2, k4.
Row 5: P3, 3-St RPC, p4.
Row 6: K5, p2, k3.
Row 7: P2, 3-St RPC, p5.
Row 8: K6, p2, k2.
Row 9: P2, 3-St LPC, p1, MB, p3.
Row 10: K5, p2, k3.
Row 11: P3, 3-St LPC, p4.
Row 12: K4, p2, k4.
Row 13: P4, 3-St LPC, p3.
Row 14: K3, p2, k5.
Row 15: P5, 3-St LPC, p2.
Row 16: K2, p2, k6.
Repeat rows 1 – 16.

CLAW CABLE

I don't like calling this a claw cable—that sounds scary. It's soft and pretty so I much prefer paw or double. Whatever you call it, the cable can be worked in either an upward or downward direction.

BASIC PATTERN
Multiple of 12 stitches with 4 edge stitches *(OPTIONAL)*

UPWARD CLAW
AS SHOWN ON RIGHT SIDE OF SWATCH

- ☐ Knit on RS, purl on WS
- ⊟ Purl on RS, knit on WS
- ▱ 6-St RKC
- ▱ 6-St LKC

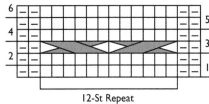

12-St Repeat

Row 1(RS): P2, k12, p2.
Row 2: K2, p12, k2.
Row 3: P2, 6-St RKC, 6-St LKC, p2.
Row 4: K2, p12, k2.
Rows 5: P2, k12, p2.
Row 6: K2, p12, k2.
Repeat rows 1 – 6.

- -

DOWNWARD CLAW

- ☐ Knit on RS, purl on WS
- ⊟ Purl on RS, knit on WS
- ▱ 6-St RKC
- ▱ 6-St LKC

12-St Repeat

AS SHOWN ON LEFT SIDE OF SWATCH
Row 1(RS): P2, k12, p2.
Row 2: K2, p12, k2.
Row 3: P2, 6-St LKC, 6 St RKC, p2.
Row 4: K2, p12, k2.
Rows 5: P2, k12, p2.
Row 6: K2, p12, k2.
Repeat rows 1 – 6.

PLAITED CABLE

This cable looks complicated but, in fact, it's easy to work. An 8-stitch cable is alternated from side to side within a 12-stitch band. The appearance of the cable varies depending on which direction the starting cable is worked.

BASIC PATTERN
Multiple of 12 stitches with 4 edge stitches *(optional)*

OUTWARD PLAIT
As Shown On Left Side Of Swatch

☐ Knit on RS, purl on WS
⊟ Purl on RS, knit on WS
⬳ 8-St RKC
⬳ 8-St LKC

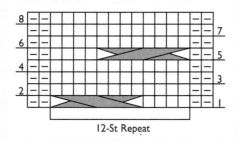

12-St Repeat

Row 1 (RS): P2, k4, 8-St LKC, p2.
Row 2: K2, p12, k2.
Row 3: P2, k12, p2.
Row 4: K2, p12, k2.
Row 5: P2, 8-St RKC, k4, p2.
Row 6: K2, p12, k2.
Row 7: P2, k12, p2.
Row 8: K2, p12, k2.
Repeat rows 1 – 8.

INWARD PLAIT
As Shown On Right Side Of Swatch

☐ Knit on RS, purl on WS
⊟ Purl on RS, knit on WS
⬳ 8-St RKC
⬳ 8-St LKC

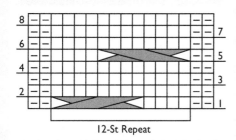

12-St Repeat

Row 1 (RS): P2, k4, 8-St RKC, p2.
Row 2: K2, p12, k2.
Row 3: P2, k12, p2.
Row 4: K2, p12, k2.
Row 5: P2, 8-St LKC, k4, p2.
Row 6: K2, p12, k2.
Row 7: P2, k12, p2.
Row 8: K2, p12, k2.
Repeat rows 1 – 8.

TWISTED CHAIN CABLE

In this cable pattern, basic cables meander in and out of each other to create a fascinating design. The result looks like a beautiful chain.

BASIC PATTERN
Multiple of 16 stitches with 4 edge stitches *(optional)*

☐ Knit on RS, purl on WS
⊟ Purl on RS, knit on WS
▨ 4-St RPC
▨ 4-St LKC
▨ 4-St LPC

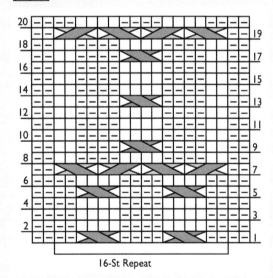

16-St Repeat

Row 1 (RS): P4, [4-St LKC, p4] twice.
Row 2: K4, [p4, k4] twice.
Row 3: P4, [k4, p4] twice.
Row 4: K4, [p4, k4] twice.
Row 5: P4, [4-St LKC, p4] twice.
Row 6: K4, [p4, k4] twice.
Row 7: P2, [4-St RPC, 4-St LPC] twice, p2.
Row 8: K2, p2, k4, p4, k4, p2, k2.
Row 9: P2, k2, p4, 4-St LKC, p4, k2, p2.
Row 10: K2, p2, k4, p4, k4, p2, k2.
Row 11: P2, k2, p4, k4, p4, k2, p2.
Row 12: K2, p2, k4, p4, k4, p2, k2.
Row 13: P2, k2, p4, 4-St LKC, p4, k2, p2.
Row 14: K2, p2, k4, p4, k4, p2, k2.
Row 15: P2, k2, p4, k4, p4, k2, p2.
Row 16: K2, p2, k4, p4, k4, p2, k2.
Row 17: P2, k2, p4, 4-St LKC, p4, k2, p2.
Row 18: K2, p2, k4, p4, k4, p2, k2.
Row 19: P2, [4-St LPC, 4-St RPC] twice, p2.
Row 20: K4, [p4, k4] twice.
Repeat rows 1 – 20.

DANCING CIRCLES CABLE

A series of simple cables combine to make this lively design. The middle section of 16 stitches, marked with heavy lines, is repeated until the desired width is reached. The sections outside the heavy lines are used only once to complete the side edges. The stitch count on the edges changes but the two sides combined always equal 8 stitches.

BASIC PATTERN
Multiple of 16 stitches plus 8 edge stitches
Directions related to the center 16-St Repeat section are in parentheses.

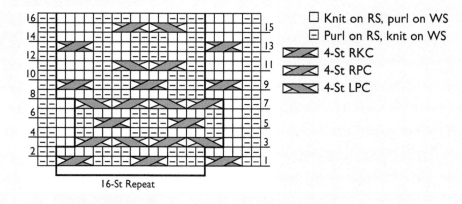

16-St Repeat

☐ Knit on RS, purl on WS
⊟ Purl on RS, knit on WS
▨ 4-St RKC
▨ 4-St RPC
▨ 4-St LPC

Row 1 (RS): P2, 4-St RKC, [p4, 4-St RKC] twice, p2.
Row 2: K2, [p4, k4] twice, p4, k2.
Row 3: P2, k2, [4-St LPC, 4-St RPC] twice, k2, p2.
Row 4: K2, p2, [k2, p4, k2] twice, p2, k2.
Row 5: P2, k2, [p2, 4-St RKC, p2] twice, k2, p2.
Row 6: K2, p2, [k2, p4, k2] twice, p2, k2.
Row 7: P2, k2, [4-St RPC, 4-St LPC] twice, p2, k2.
Row 8: K2, [p4, k4] twice, p4, k2.

Row 9: P2, 4-St RKC, [p4, 4-St RKC] twice, p2.
Row 10: K2, [p4, k4] twice, p4, k2.
Row 11: P2, k4, p2, 4-St RPC, 4-St LPC, p2, k4, p2.
Row 12: K2, p4, k2, p2, k4, p2, k2, p4, k2.
Row 13: P2, 4-St RKC, p2, k2, p4, k2, p2, 4-St RKC, p2.
Row 14: K2, p4, k2, p2, k4, p2, k2, p4, k2.
Row 15: P2, k4, p2, 4-St LPC, 4-St RPC, p2, k4, p2.
Row 16: K2, [p4, k4] twice, p4, k2.
Repeat rows 1 – 16.

LAPTOP COVER

My computer is my baby! It goes everywhere with me and I wanted a cover that would keep it padded but look great. In this design, hand painted wool is combined with an interesting multifiber bouclé yarn.

FINISHED MEASUREMENTS
10" wide × 15" long (25.4 × 38.1 cm)

GAUGE
12 stitches and 17 rows = 4" (10 cm) in stockinette stitch
16 stitches and 20 rows = 4" (10 cm) in cable pattern

MATERIALS
Yarn A: Medium weight hand painted wool yarn,
approx 300 yd (274 m)
Yarn B: Medium weight multi fiber bouclé yarn,
approx 135 yd (123 m)

NEEDLES AND NOTIONS
Size 11 (8 mm) knitting needles or size necessary to obtain correct gauge
Cable needle
Yarn needle for weaving in ends
Four buttons, 1" (2.5 cm) diameter with large holes and no shank

BEGINNING SECTION

First make the buttonholes on the front and establish the rib pattern in preparation for the main section. This section is made with two strands of the wool (Yarn A) held together.

BUTTONHOLE CHART

☐ Knit on RS, purl on WS
⊟ Purl on RS, knit on WS
⊠ K2tog in knit stitches; P2tog in purl stitches
⊙ Yarn Over (yo)

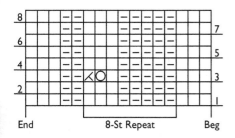

With 2 strands of Yarn A held together, cast on 40 stitches.
Row 1 (RS): K3, [p5, k3] 4 times, p2, k3.
Row 2: P3, k2, [p3, k5] 4 times, p3.
Row 3: K3, [p5, k1, yo, k2tog] 4 times, p2, k3.
Row 4: P3, k2, [p3, k5] 4 times, p3.
Row 5: K3, [p5, k3] 4 times, p2, k3.
Row 6: P3, k2, [p3, k5] 4 times, p3.
Row 7: K3, [p5, k3] 4 times, p2, k3.
Row 8: P3, k2, [p3, k5] 4 times, p3.

MAIN SECTION

The main section is knit with one strand each of the wool (Yarn A) and bouclé (Yarn B). The squiggles and bumps chart is repeated four times.

Cut 1 strand of Yarn A and replace it with 1 strand of Yarn B. Use 1 strand of Yarn A and Yarn B held together for the Main Section.

LAP TOP COVER CHART

☐ Knit on RS, purl on WS
⊟ Purl on RS, knit on WS
⦿ MB
▨ 3-St RPC
▨ 3-St LPC

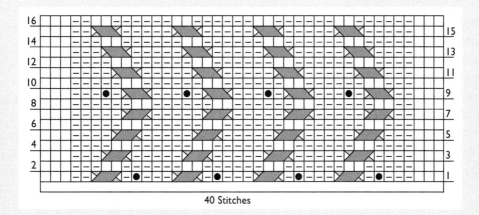

40 Stitches

IN THIS PATTERN, the stitches that precede the bobble are purl stitches, so be sure to move your yarn to the back before you start working on the bobble.

Row 1 (RS): K3, [p3, MB, p1, 3-St RPC] 4 times, p2, k3.
Row 2: P3, [k3, p2, k3] 4 times, k2, p3.
Row 3: K3, [p4, 3-St RPC, p1] 4 times, p2, k3.
Row 4: P3, k2, [k2, p2, k4] 4 times, p3.
Row 5: K3, [p3, 3-St RPC, p2] 4 times, p2, k3.
Row 6: P3, k2, [k3, p2, k3] 4 times, p3.
Row 7: K3, [p2, 3-St RPC, p3] 4 times, p2, k3.
Row 8: P3, k2, [k4, p2, k2] 4 times, p3.
Row 9: K3, [p2, 3-St LPC, p1, MB, p1] 4 times, p2, k3.
Row 10: P3, k2, [k3, p2, k3] 4 times, p3.
Row 11: K3, [p3, 3-St LPC, p2] 4 times, p2, k3.
Row 12: P3, k2, [k2, p2, k4] 4 times, p3.
Row 13: K3, [p4, 3-St LPC, p1] 4 times, p2, k3.
Row 14: P3, [k3, p2, k3] 4 times, k2, p3.
Row 15: K3, [p5, 3-St LPC] 4 times, p2, k3.
Row 16: P3, k2, [p2, k6] 4 times, p3.
Repeat rows 1 – 16 (4 times more).

ENDING SECTION

The ending section makes the back of the laptop case. The design continues with a plain rib that echoes the pattern on the front and also switches back to two strands of wool (Yarn A). *Note:* The back section is intentionally a bit shorter than the front section.

Cut the strand of Yarn B and replace with a second strand of Yarn A.
Row 1 (RS): K3, [p5, k3] 4 times, p2, k3.
Row 2: P3, k2, [p3, k5] 4 times, p3.
Repeat rows 1 – 2 until the length from the beginning is 30" (76.2 cm).
Bind off all stitches loosely keeping to rib pattern.

TO BIND OFF in pattern, work two stitches at a time in the usual way but knit or purl the stitches following the last row of the project pattern.

MAKE BOBBLE BUTTONS

The finishing touch is created by bobble buttons that match the bobbles on the cable. *Note:* when you cut the yarn be sure and leave the tails at least 8" (20.5cm) long to assemble the bobble and sew on the backing buttons.

Make four bobble buttons.

With one strand of Yarn A and one strand of Yarn B held together, cast on 2 stitches.

K1, [k1, yo, k1, yo, k1] all into next stitch. You have 6 sts on the needle.

Working just the 5 stitches that have been made from the one stitch, turn, purl 5, turn, knit 5.

Turn, [p2tog] (3 times).

Turn, slip 1 st, k2tog, pass the slipped stitch over the stitch just worked. Cut yarn, leaving at least 8" (20.5 cm), and pull through last loop to fasten off.

Thread one strand of yarn from the tail on a yarn needle and work a running stitch around open edge of bobble. If desired, stuff a tiny ball of waste yarn into center of bobble, pull running stitch tight. Knot all four strands.

ASSEMBLING THE LAP TOP COVER

Fold the cover in half, wrong sides together, so the ribbed section is the back and the Cabled section is the front. Line up the short sides and invisibly stitch the long side seams.

ATTACH BUTTONS

The buttons are attached to the wrong side of the back (inside the case) opposite the buttonholes on the front.

Mark the location for the buttons.

Thread two strands of the yarn from bottom of bobble onto the tapestry needle.

Pass yarn from the inside to the outside of the Lap Top Cover. Repeat with the other two strands.

Working from outside, thread the yarn through holes on the backing button.

Tie a sturdy square knot and trim yarn ends to desired length.

FINISHING

Using a tapestry needle, weave in all ends. It is not necessary to block.

COZY PILLOW

The dancing circles cable is a natural choice to make a pillow. Chunky alpaca is knit using large needles so the project is finished quickly. This particular yarn is hand dyed and the color variation adds an unusual depth to the design.

FINISHED MEASUREMENTS
18" (45.7 cm) square after sewing
18" wide x 38" long (45.7 x 97cm) before sewing

GAUGE
13 stitches and 17 rows = 4" (10 cm) in stockinette stitch on larger needle
20 stitches and 19 rows = 4" (10 cm) in cable pattern

MATERIALS
Bulky weight hand-dyed alpaca yarn, approx 525 yd (480 m)

NEEDLES AND NOTIONS
Size 9 (6 mm) knitting needles or size necessary to obtain gauge
Size 10½ (6.5 mm) knitting needles
Cable needle
Yarn needle for weaving in ends
18" (45.7 cm) square pillow form
Three buttons, 1" (2.5 cm) diameter

SETUP ROWS

First, work a 6-row section with a garter stitch border. Several increases will set up your knitting to work the main section.

Using smaller needles, cast on 67 stitches.
Row 1 (RS): Knit.
Row 2: Knit.
Row 3: K3, *inc 1, k5 *; repeat from * to * until last 4 sts, inc 1, k3—78 sts.
Row 4: K2, p4, * k3, p4 *; repeat from * to * until last 2 sts, k2.
Change to larger needles.
Row 5: P2, 4-St RKC, *p3, 4-St RKC *; repeat from * to * until last 2 sts, p2.
Row 6: K2, p4, *k1, inc 1, k1, p4 *; repeat from * to * until last 2 sts, k2— 88 sts.

MAIN SECTION
PILLOW COVER CHART

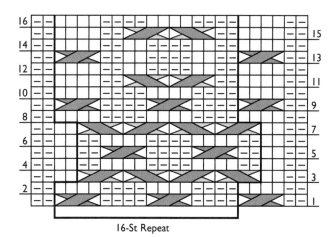

- □ Knit on RS, purl on WS
- ⊟ Purl on RS, knit on WS
- 4-St RKC
- 4-St RPC
- 4-St LPC

16-St Repeat

Repeat the Dancing Circles pattern over and over until your piece measures about 36" (91.4 cm) in length. If the piece is too short after the given number of rows, then work another repeat. Since the knitted fabric will be overlapped, it's ok to be longer; it's not ok to be shorter. To be absolutely certain that your knitting is long enough, measure it on the pillow. It should wrap around completely with an overlap of at least 2" (5.1 cm).

Row 1 (RS): P2, 4-St RKC, *p4, 4-St RKC*; repeat from * to * until last 2 sts, p2.
Row 2: K2, *p4, k4*; repeat from * to * until last 6 sts, p4, k2.
Row 3: P2, k2, *4-St LPC, 4-St RPC*; repeat from * to * until last 4 sts, k2, p2.
Row 4: K2, p2, *k2, p4, k2*; repeat from * to * until last 4 sts, p2, k2.
Row 5: P2, k2, *p2, 4-St RKC, p2*; repeat from * to * until last 4 sts, k2, p2.
Row 6: K2, p2, *k2, p4, k2*; repeat from * to * until last 4 sts, p2, k2.
Row 7: P2, k2, *4-St RPC, 4-St LPC*; repeat from * to * until last 4 sts, k2, p2.
Row 8: K2, *p4, k4*; repeat from * to * until last 6 sts, p4, k2.
Row 9: P2, 4-St RKC, *p4, 4-St RKC*; repeat from * to * until last 2 sts, p2.
Row 10: K2, *p4, k4*; repeat from * to * until last 6 sts, p4, k2.
Row 11: P2, k4, *p2, 4-St RPC, 4-St LPC, p2 k4*; repeat from * to * until last 2 sts, p2.
Row 12: K2, *p4, k2, p2, k4, p2, k2*; repeat from * to *until last 6 sts, p4, k2.
Row 13: P2, 4-St RKC, *p2, k2, p4, k2, p2, 4-St RKC*; repeat from * to *until last 2 sts, p2.
Row 14: K2, *p4, k2, p2, k4, p2, k2*; repeat from * to * until last 6 sts, p4, k2.
Row 15: P2, k4, *p2, 4-St LPC, 4-St RPC, p2, k4*; repeat from * to *until last 2 sts, p2.
Row 16: K2, *p4, k4*; repeat from * to * until last 6 sts, p4, k2.
Repeat rows 1 – 16 (10 more times), then work rows 1 – 9.

Finally, work a second garter stitch band containing some decreases and three buttonholes.

Row 1 (WS): K2, p4, *k1, k2tog, k1, p4 *; repeat from * to * until last 2 sts, k2 – 78 sts.
Row 2: P2, 4-St RKC, *p3, 4-St RKC; repeat from * to * until last 2 sts, p2.
Row 3: K3, k2tog, *k5, k2tog*; repeat from * to * until last 3 sts, k3 – 67 sts.
Change to smaller needles.
Row 4 *(Make buttonholes)*: [K15, k2tog, yo] 3 times, k16.
Row 5: Knit across.
Bind off all stitches in pattern.

FINISHING

Using the tapestry needle, weave in all ends.

If desired, lightly steam block using a steam iron on a wool setting. Don't let the iron actually touch the knitting.

With right side of the knitting facing the right side of the pillow, wrap the strip around the pillow so the short ends overlap in the center of the pillow. Make sure that the finishing band with the buttonholes is touching the pillow with the other band on top (closest to you). Remember, you are working with the pillow cover inside out at this point. Without catching the pillow, pin each side in 5 or 6 places. Then gently remove the pillow form.

Using yarn threaded on a yarn needle, sew the sides using a backstitch. The overlap will be in the center of the seam. When you get to this point, sew through all the layers, checking frequently that you are catching all three layers.

Turn pillow cover right side out and mark button locations under the buttonholes. Sew on three buttons. If desired, use a small square of wool felt on the backside of the button so your stitches don't pull through the knitting.

Insert pillow form and button closed.

KNITTING ABBREVIATIONS

cm	centimeters
dec	decrease
g	grams
k	knit
inc	knit into front and back loop of same stitch or purl into front and back loop of same stitch
k2tog	knit two stitches together
MB	make bobble
M1	increase 1 by inserting the left hand needle under the horizontal thread between the stitch just worked and the next st; knit into the back of the resulting loop to make a stitch
mm	millimeters
p	purl
p2tog	purl two stitches together
psso	pass slipped st over
RS	right side
sl	slip
ssk	slip the first and second stitches one at a time kwise, then insert left hand needle into the fronts of these stitches and knit them together.
st(s)	stitch(es)
St st	Stockinette stitch (k on RS, p on WS)
WS	wrong side
yo	yarn over needle
*	repeat instructions between * as directed
[ ]	repeat instructions enclosed by brackets as directed

CPSIA information can be obtained at www.ICGtesting.com
Printed in the USA
LVOW02s2348120715

445797LV00005B/6/P